Squirrels

Leo Statts

abdopublishing.com

Published by Abdo Zoom™, PO Box 398166, Minneapolis, Minnesota 55439. Copyright © 2018 by Abdo Consulting Group, Inc. International copyrights reserved in all countries. No part of this book may be reproduced in any form without written permission from the publisher. Abdo Zoom™ is a trademark and logo of Abdo Consulting Group, Inc.

Printed in the United States of America, North Mankato, Minnesota
052017
092017

THIS BOOK CONTAINS
RECYCLED MATERIALS

Cover Photo: Neil Burton/iStockphoto
Interior Photos: Shutterstock Images, 1; iStockphoto, 5, 8–9, 10, 14–15, 16, 18–19; Abi Warner/iStockphoto, 6; Puttinan Inchan/Shutterstock Images, 7; Red Line Editorial, 9, 20 (left), 20 (right), 21 (left), 21 (right); Y. Helfman/iStockphoto, 10–11; Nathan Giftu/iStockphoto, 13; Sue Feldberg/iStockphoto, 14; Robert Eastman/Shutterstock Images, 17

Editor: Brienna Rossiter
Series Designer: Madeline Berger
Art Direction: Dorothy Toth

Publishers Cataloging-in-Publication Data
Names: Statts, Leo, author.
Title: Squirrels / by Leo Statts.
Description: Minneapolis, MN : Abdo Zoom, 2018. | Series: Backyard animals |
    Includes bibliographical references and index.
Identifiers: LCCN 2017931123 | ISBN 9781532120060 (lib. bdg.) |
    ISBN 9781614797173 (ebook) | ISBN 9781614797739 (Read-to-me ebook)
Subjects: LCSH: Squirrels--Juvenile literature. | Rodents--Juvenile literature.
Classification: DDC 599.36--dc23
LC record available at http://lccn.loc.gov/2017931123

Table of Contents

Squirrels

Squirrels are **rodents**. They have long, bushy tails. There are many kinds of squirrels.

Squirrels can be many colors and sizes. They have big eyes.

6

Their front teeth are large.

Squirrels live in many places around the world. They live in **grasslands** and forests. Some even live in **arctic** areas.

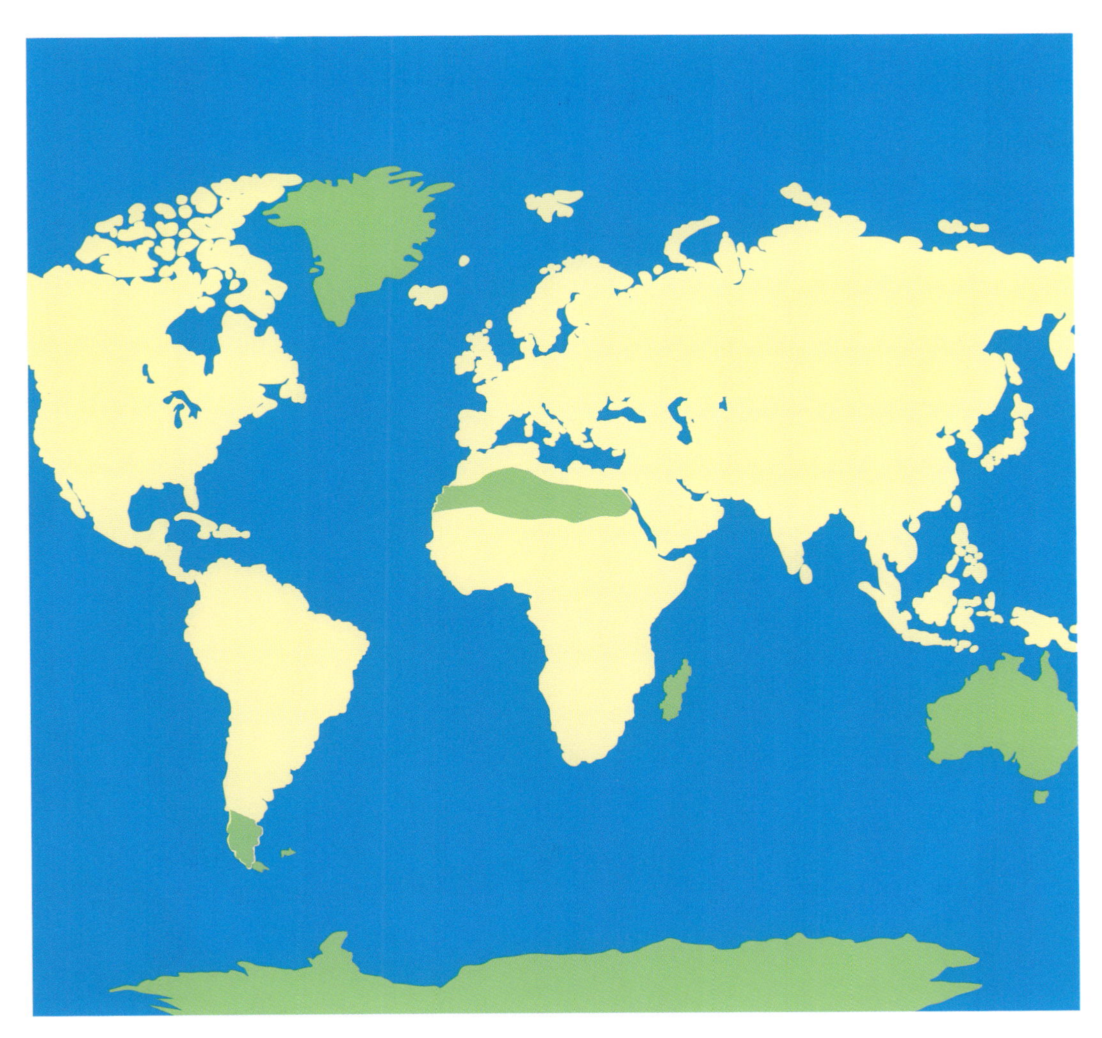

Where squirrels live

Some squirrels make nests in trees.

Others dig homes in the ground.

Squirrels mostly eat nuts, seeds, and **grains**. Sometimes they eat eggs and insects.

Squirrels **forage** for food.

They eat some food right away.
They store the rest for winter.

Life Cycle

Squirrels are
born in nests or
holes in trees.

Baby squirrels
are tiny and **blind**.
Their mother takes
care of them.

Later on, the baby squirrels leave the nest. They find their own homes.

Some squirrels
live alone, but
others live in
groups. Squirrels
can live up to
14 years.

Average Length – Shortest

An American pygmy squirrel is shorter than a basketball.

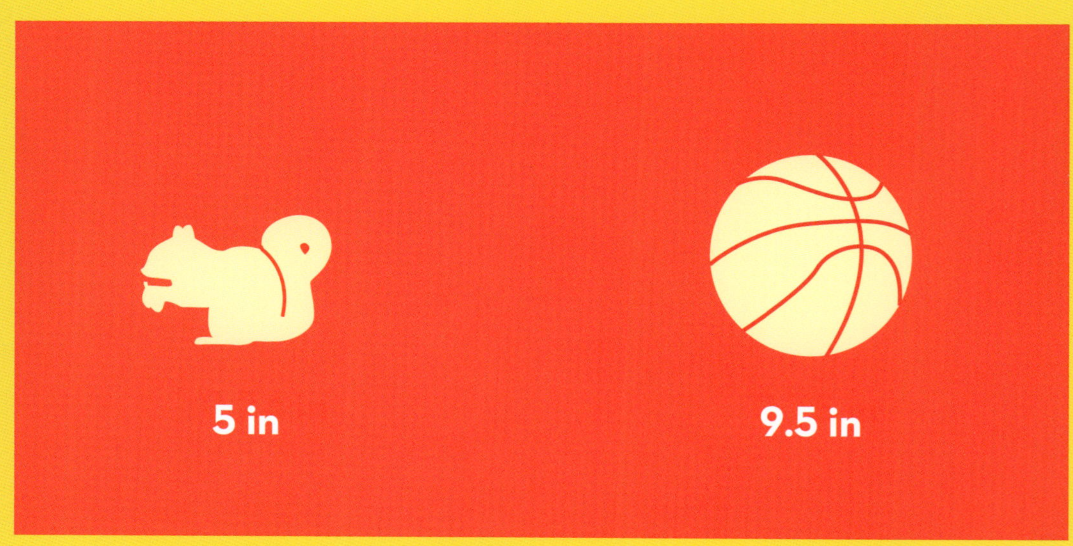

Average Length – Longest

An Indian giant squirrel is longer than a basketball.

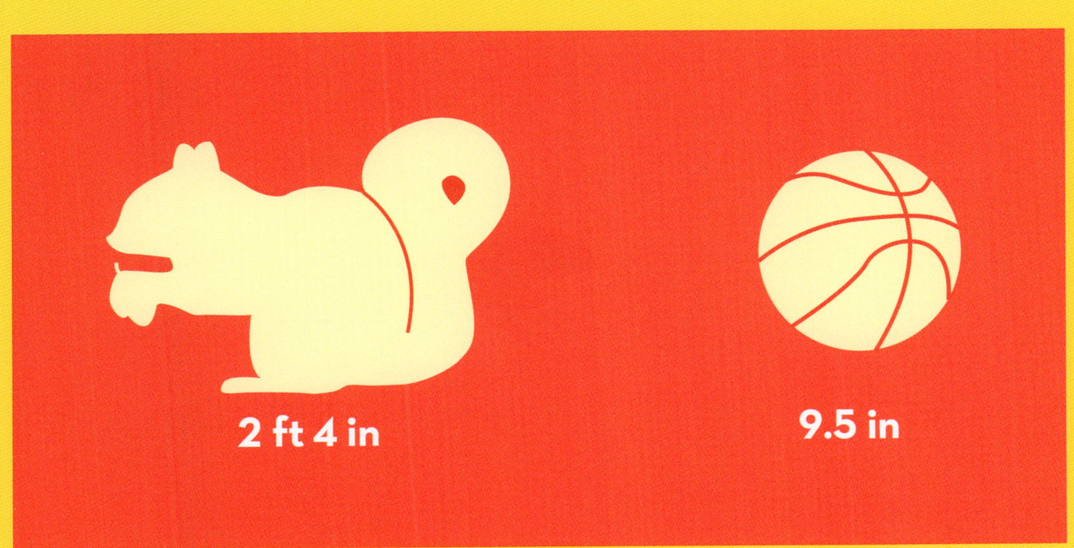

Glossary

arctic – from the cold area around the North Pole.

blind – unable to see.

forage – to search, especially for food.

grains – the seeds of plants that are used for food.

grassland – a large area of grass, with few or no trees.

rodent – a small animal with large front teeth.

Booklinks

For more information on **squirrels**, please visit abdobooklinks.com

Learn even more with the Abdo Zoom Animals database. Check out **abdozoom.com** for more information.

Index